VOCAL SELECTIONS
THE LIFE

Music by
CY COLEMAN

Lyrics by
IRA GASMAN

Cover photo: Serino Coyne

ISBN 978-1-4234-9832-2

7777 W. BLUEMOUND RD. P.O. BOX 13819 MILWAUKEE, WI 53213

For info on Notable Music Co. Inc./The Cy Coleman Office, visit
www.cycoleman.com and **www.myspace.com/cycoleman**

Visit Hal Leonard Online at
www.halleonard.com

CONTENTS

CY COLEMAN

Cy Coleman was a musician's composer, classically trained at piano, composition, and orchestration at New York City's High School for the Performing Arts and NY College of Music. Mr. Coleman was being groomed to be the next great conductor. Instead he turned his passion to jazz and formed the popular Cy Coleman Trio. Born Seymour Kaufman on June 14, 1929 in the Bronx, he changed his name at age 16 in time to use it on his first compositions with lyricist Joe A. McCarthy ("Why Try to Change Me Now," and "I'm Gonna Laugh You Right Out of My Life"). While still performing in jazz clubs and enjoying a successful recording career, Cy began writing with veteran songwriter Carolyn Leigh. Hits like "Witchcraft" and "The Best Is Yet to Come" were followed by their leap to Broadway with *Wildcat*, starring Lucille Ball

("Hey, Look Me Over") and then *Little Me* ("I've Got Your Number" and "Real Live Girl"). In 1966 Cy, along with legendary lyricist Dorothy Fields, triumphed with the smash hit *Sweet Charity* ("Big Spender," "If My Friends Could See Me Now"). Cy continued on Broadway and wrote the scores for *Seesaw, I Love My Wife, On the Twentieth Century, Barnum, City of Angels, The Will Rogers Follies*, and *The Life*. In 2004 Cy returned to his roots and revived the Cy Coleman Trio, once again wowing the audiences with his amazing skill at the piano. In Mr. Coleman's amazing career he took home three Tony® Awards, two GRAMMY Awards®, three Emmy® Awards, an Academy Award® nomination, and countless honors. Cy served on the Board of ASCAP for three decades.

IRA GASMAN

Ira Gasman is an American theatre writer, lyricist, and newspaper columnist.

He studied Musical Theatre with Aaron Frankel and was an original member of the B.M.I. Music Theatre Workshop. He has written for night clubs, television, and motion pictures, collaborating with such distinguished composers—besides Cy Coleman—as Burton Lane, Jule Styne, Steve Allen, and Galt MacDermot. His songs have been recorded by Liza Minnelli, Bobby Short, Margaret Whiting, Joe Williams, and George Burns.

Gasman was nominated for Tony® and Drama Desk Awards for his contributions to *The Life*, the 1997 Broadway musical that had its first production at off-Broadway's Westbeth Theatre seven years earlier, and he wrote the highly acclaimed musical revue *What's a Nice Country Like You Doing in a State Like This?*, which played in dozens of American cities and numerous countries around the world. Other credits include *Radiant Baby,* which received a Lucille Lortel Award nomination for Outstanding Musical and *The Great Radio City Music Hall Spectacular*.

He currently writes a column for *The Sag Harbor Express*, which serves the South Fork of Long Island.

USE WHAT YOU GOT

Music by CY COLEMAN
Lyrics by IRA GASMAN

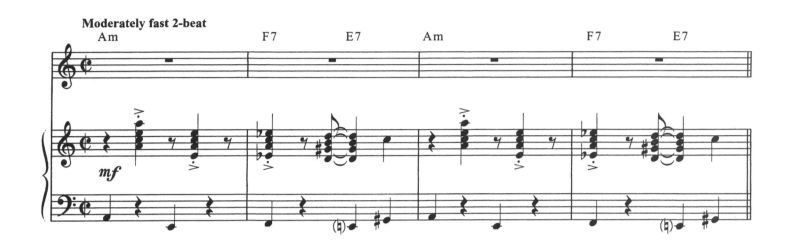

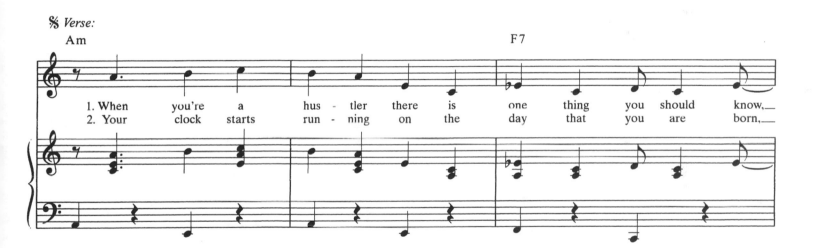

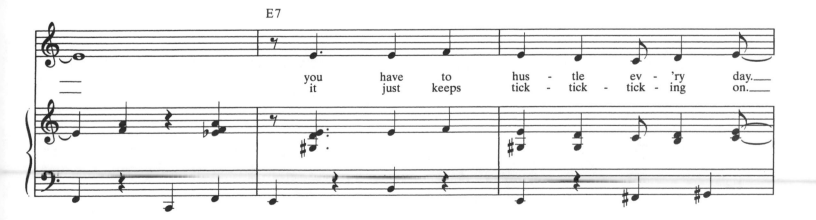

When you're a
There's on - ly

hus - tler there's no time to take it slow.____
so much time to blow your lit - tle horn.____

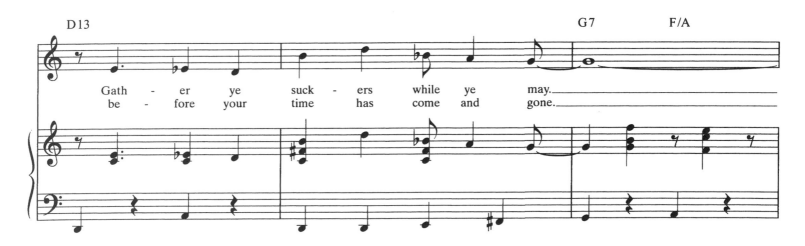

Gath - er ye suck - ers while ye may.____
be - fore your time has come and gone.____

Mon - day you're hot,____
Wednes - day you're new,____

Swing ♩ = ♪ (♫ = ♪³♪)

To Coda ⊕

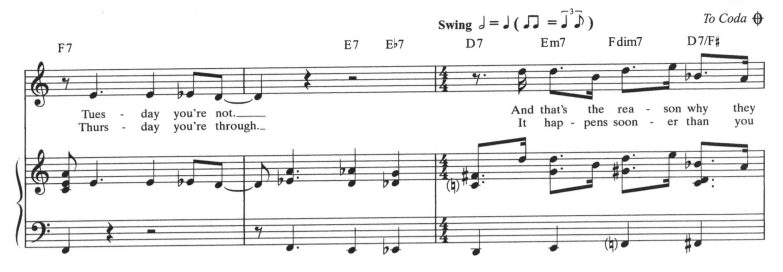

Tues - day you're not.____ And that's the rea - son why they
Thurs - day you're through._ It hap - pens soon - er than you

Chorus:

say... You got - ta use what you got____ to get what you want____ be -

fore what you got is gone._____ You got - ta reach for that ring____ while

you're on that ride.___ How long does that ride go on?_____ You got - ta

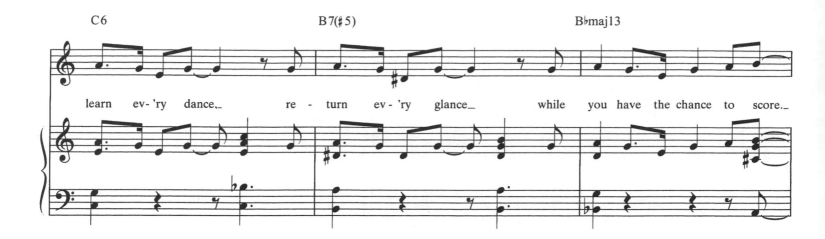

learn ev-'ry dance.___ re - turn ev-'ry glance___ while you have the chance to score.___

_____ You got - ta use what you got___ to get what you want___ be -

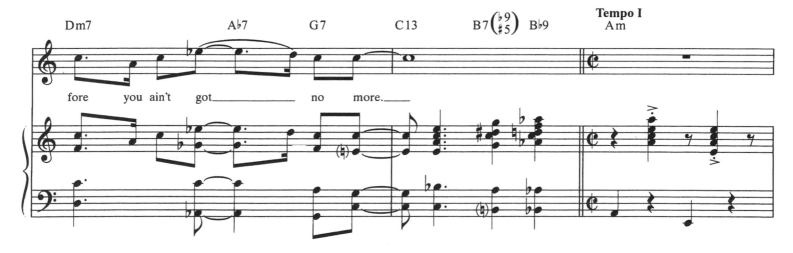

fore you ain't got_____ no more.___

Tempo I

D.S. % al Coda

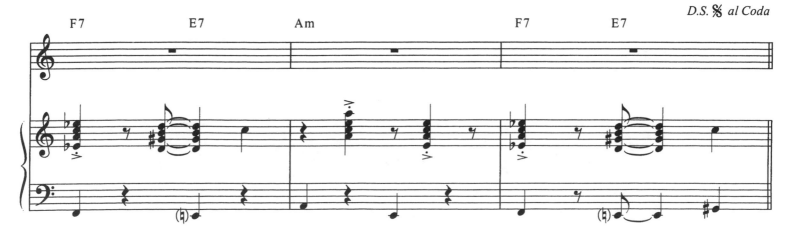

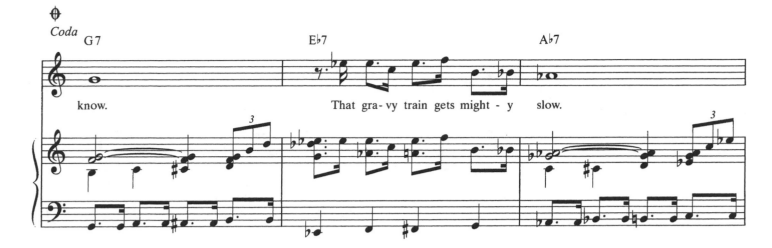

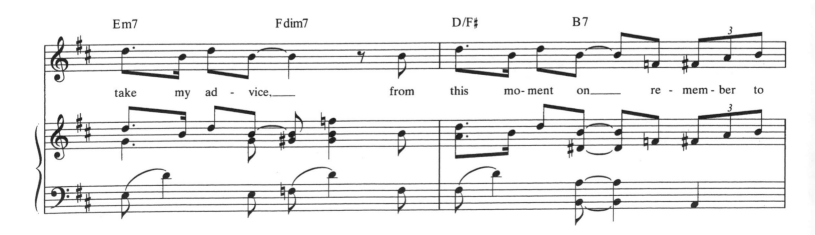

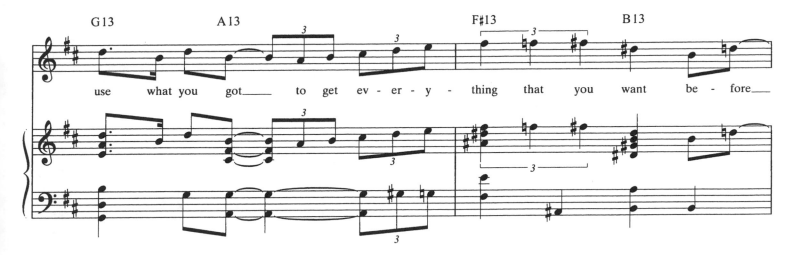

use what you got____ to get ev-er-y-thing that you want be-fore____

what you got____

is gone.____

A LOVELY DAY TO BE OUT OF JAIL

Music by CY COLEMAN
Lyrics by IRA GASMAN

Moderately

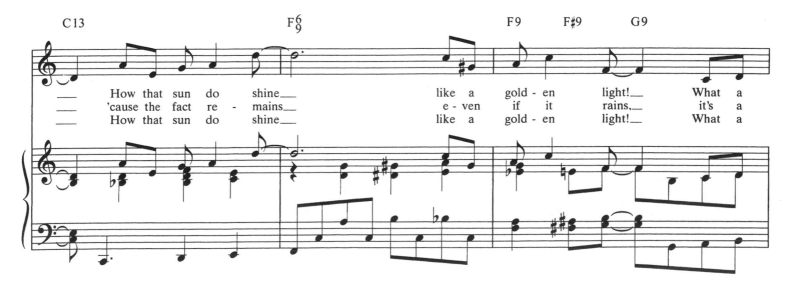

15

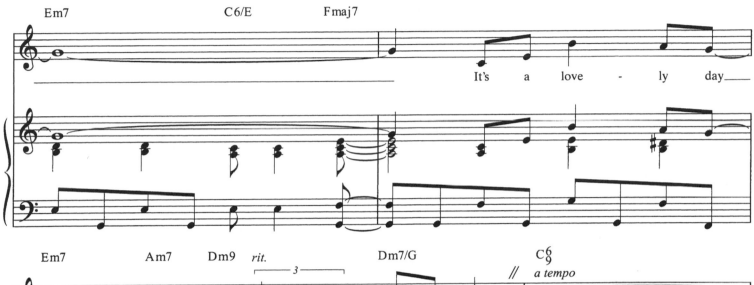

PIECE OF THE ACTION

Music by CY COLEMAN
Lyrics by IRA GASMAN

al - ways end up___ in the hole. This life I made ain't near what I ex -

pect. My dues are paid, so when do I col - lect?

Moderate funk rock ($\quarter = 84$)

§ *Verse:*

1. I wan - na piece of the ac - tion,___ I wan - na slice of the pie.___
2. I star - ted out in the gut - ter,___ I made it up to the street.___

Alternate lyric: 2. I *did my bit in the ar - my.* *I took a bul - let in 'Nam.*___
3. I wan - na piece of the high life,___ I wan - na taste of the cream.___

I wan-na get on the fast track and kiss all of this good-bye.
I got my eye on a pent-house, a neat lit-tle pent-house suite.
When I got back to Sa-van-nah, hell, no-bod-y gave a damn.
I wan-na play in the big league and be on the win-ning team.

It's time for up-ping the an-te, it's time for rais-in' the stakes.
(2.3.) I'm gon-na go for the glo-ry, I'm gon-na shoot for the moon.
I tried to find me a good job. I wore out two pairs of shoes.

To Coda ⊕ | 1.

I got the looks and the ta-lent, I got what-ev-er it takes.
I wan-na piece of the ac-tion and
I an-swered ten thou-sand want ads. Yes,

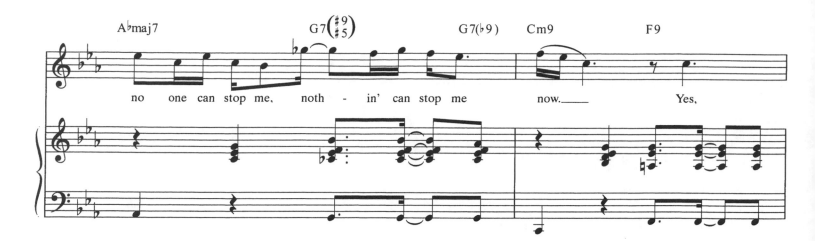

no one can stop me, noth - in' can stop me now.____ Yes,

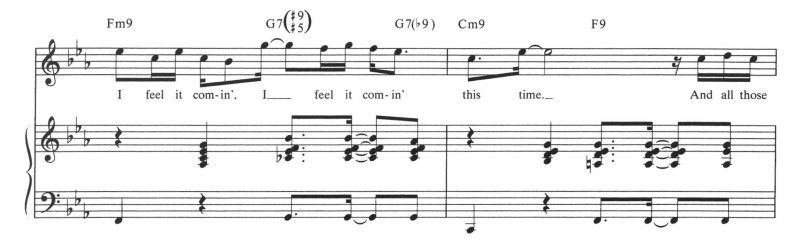

I feel it com-in', I____ feel it com-in' this time.__ And all those

two - bit tricks can go__ take a walk, I got dreams as big__ as New York.__

* Alternate melody.

THE OLDEST PROFESSION

Music by CY COLEMAN
Lyrics by IRA GASMAN

Lazy jazz waltz (♩=80)

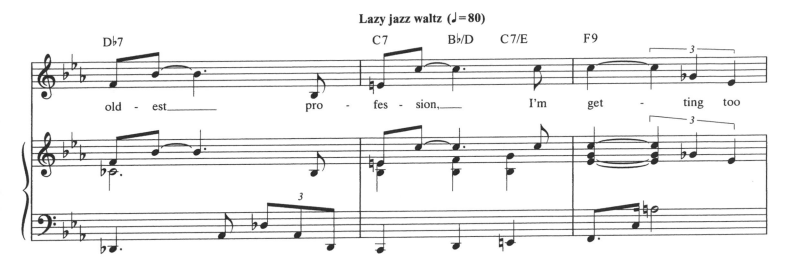

old - est_____ pro - fes - sion,_____ I'm get - ting too

tired____ and too slow._____ I'm

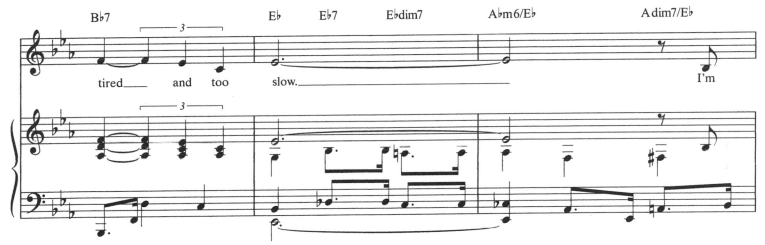

get - ting____ too old for____ the half - hour____

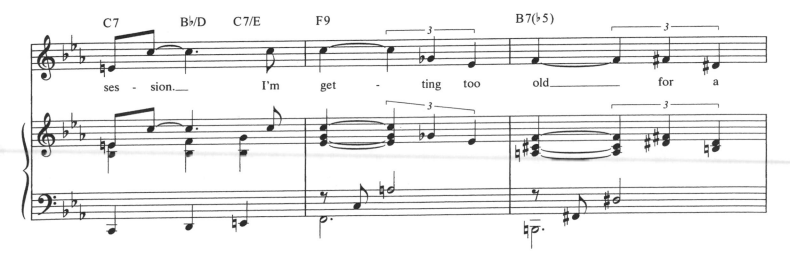

ses - sion.___ I'm get - ting too old_____ for a

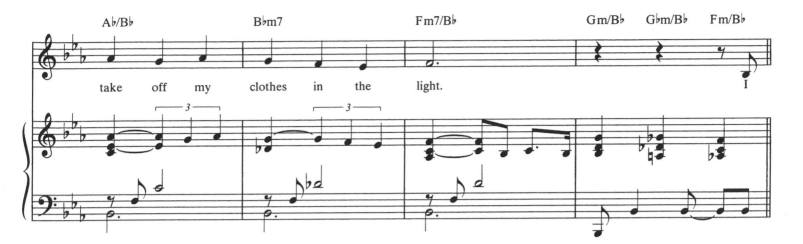

take off my clothes in the light. I

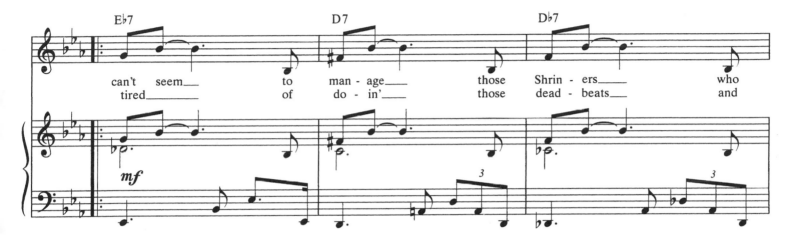

can't seem____ to man-age____ those Shrin-ers____ who
tired____ of do-in' those dead-beats____ and

man - age____ to man - han - dle me____ ev - 'ry
pik - ers____ and hag gl - ing o - ver the

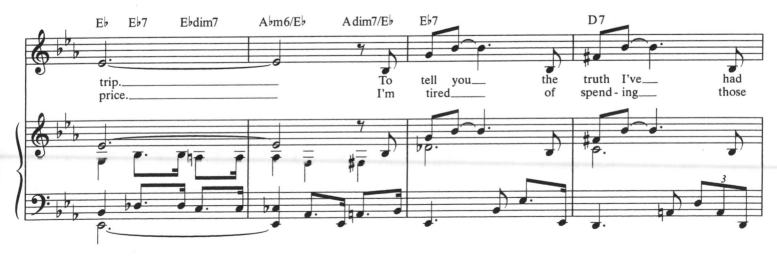

trip.____ To tell you____ the truth I've____ had
price.____ I'm tired____ of spend-ing____ those

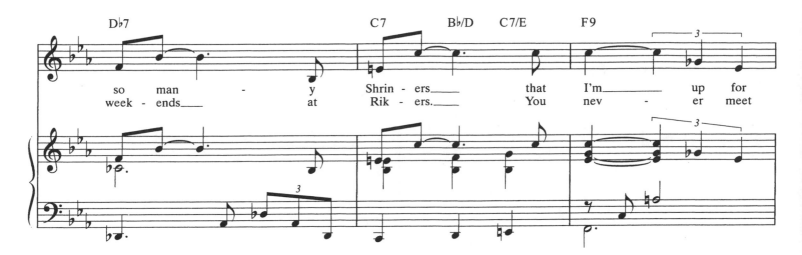

so man - y Shrin - ers____ that I'm____ up for
week - ends____ at Rik - ers.____ You nev - er meet

mem - ber - ship._____ When
an - y - one nice._____ I've

I____ was six - teen____ it was fun turn - ing
done____ ev - 'ry - thing____ that a bod - y can

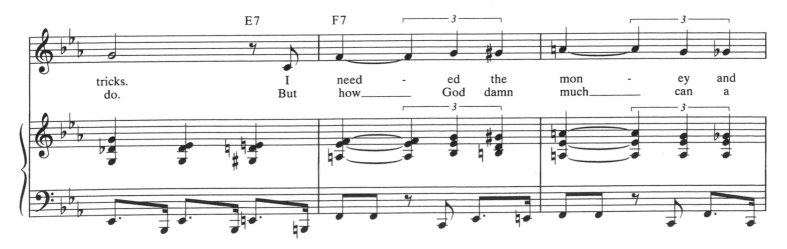

tricks. I need - ed the mon - ey and
do. But how____ God damn much____ can a

Abm6/Cb   Ab/Bb   Eb7

want - ed some kicks._____ But I ain't_____ six -
bod - y go through._____ I'm get - ting_____ too

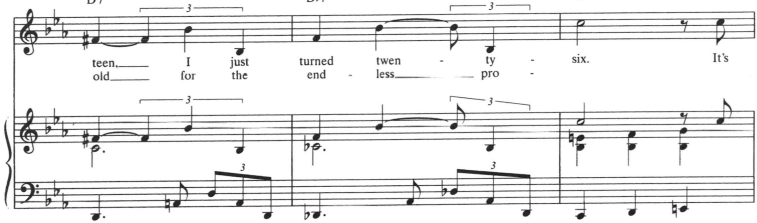

D7   Db7   1. C7 Bb/D C7/E

teen,_____ I just turned twen - ty - six. It's
old_____ for the end - less_____ pro -

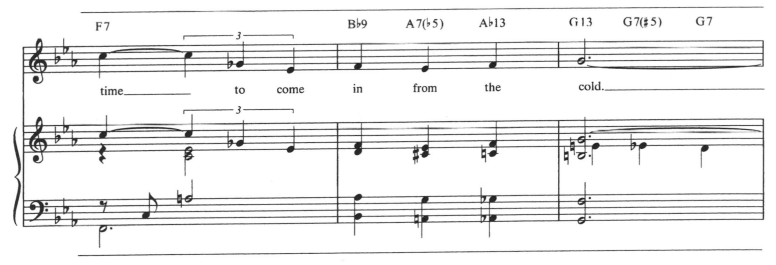

F7   Bb9 A7(b5) Ab13   G13 G7(#5) G7

time_____ to come in from the cold._____

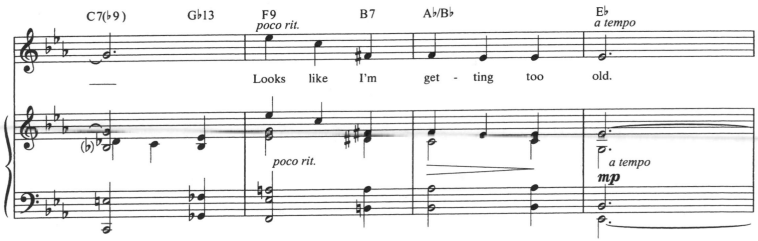

C7(b9)   Gb13   F9   B7   Ab/Bb   Eb
            poco rit.   a tempo

_____ Looks like I'm get - ting too old.

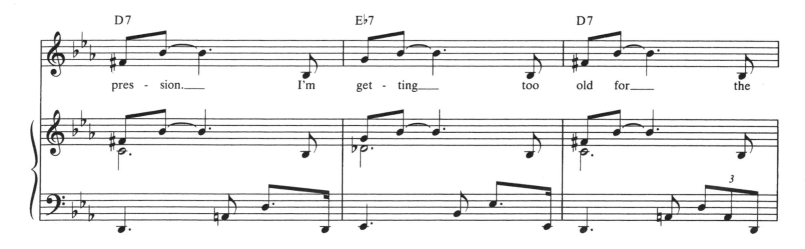

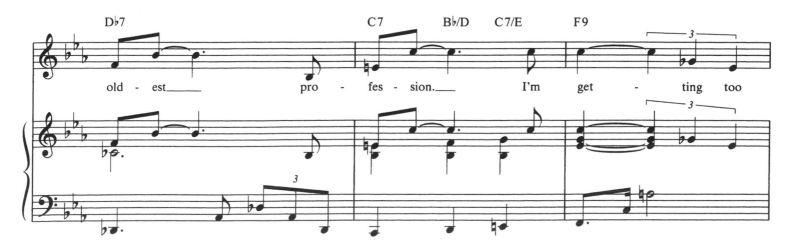

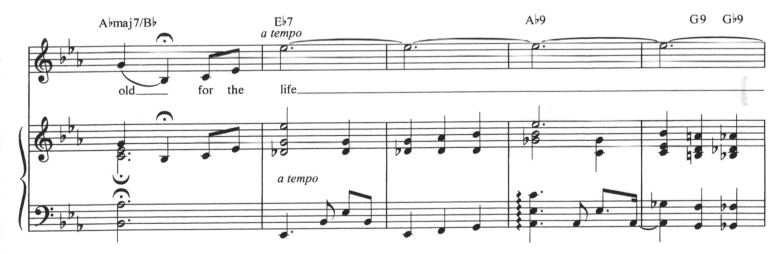

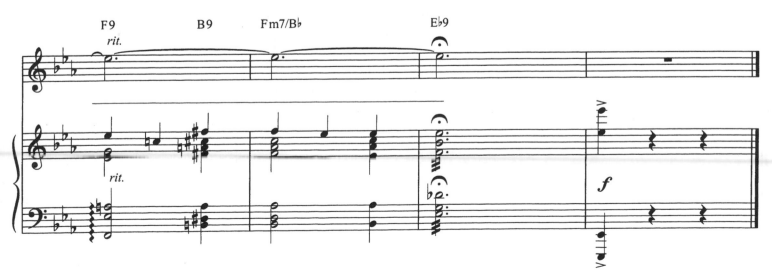

DON'T TAKE MUCH

Music by CY COLEMAN
Lyrics by IRA GASMAN

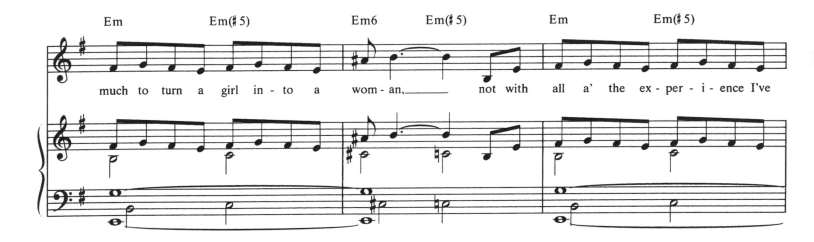

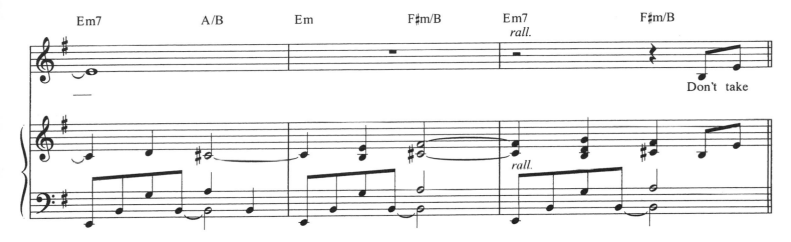

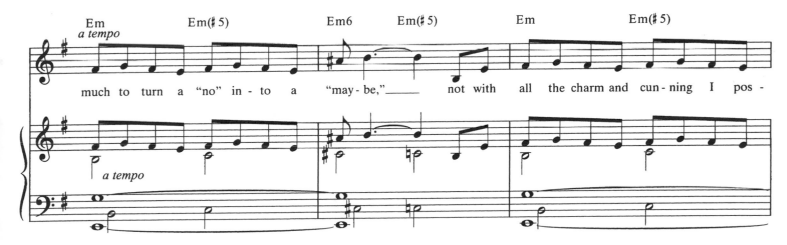

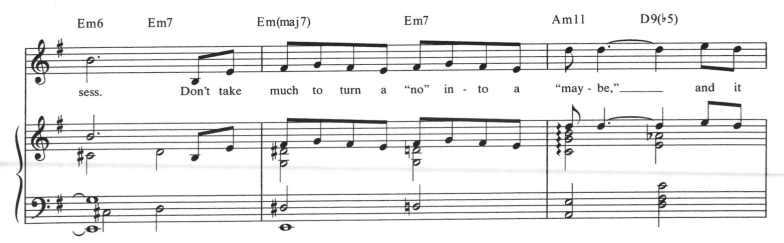

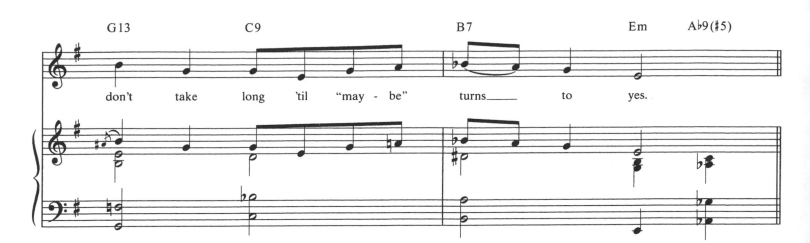

don't take long 'til "may - be" turns____ to yes.

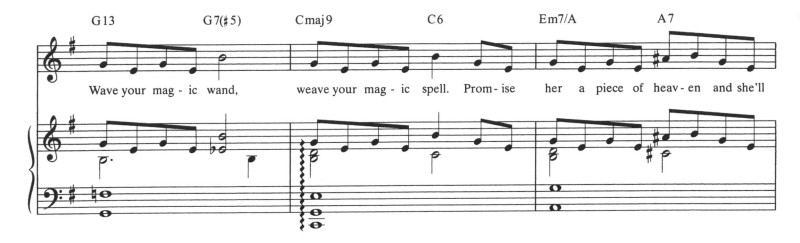

Wave your mag - ic wand, weave your mag - ic spell. Prom - ise her a piece of heav - en and she'll

fol - low you to hell. Ain't no

trick to turn a hick in - to a hook - er,____ not with all the ho - cus - po - cus that I

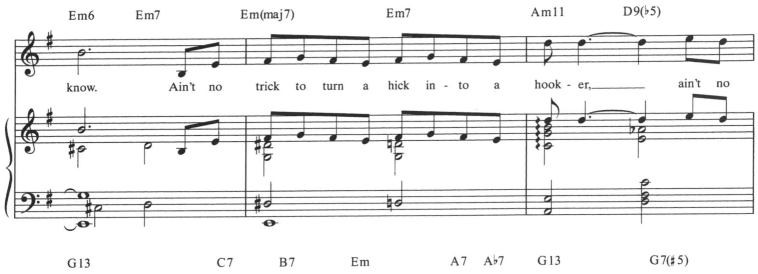

Em6 Em7 Em(maj7) Em7 Am11 D9(♭5)

know. Ain't no trick to turn a hick in - to a hook - er,____ ain't no

G13 C7 B7 Em A7 A♭7 G13 G7(♯5)

thing that I ain't done____ be - fore. All you got to do is

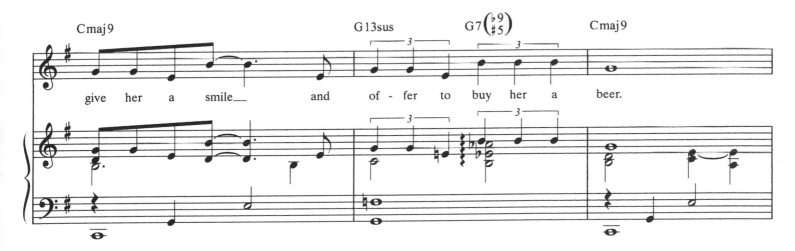

Cmaj9 G13sus G7(♭9♯5) Cmaj9

give her a smile____ and of - fer to buy her a beer.

G13 G7(♯5) Cmaj9 F♯m7(♭5) B7sus B7

All you got to do is look in her eyes____ and whis - per some lies in her

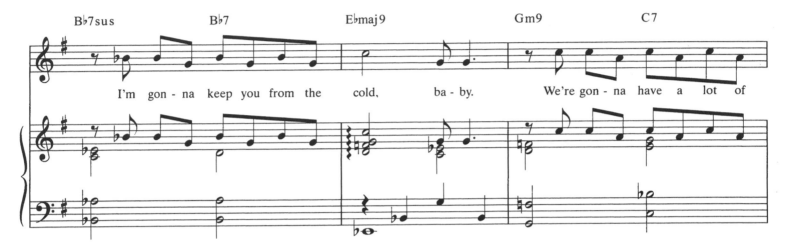

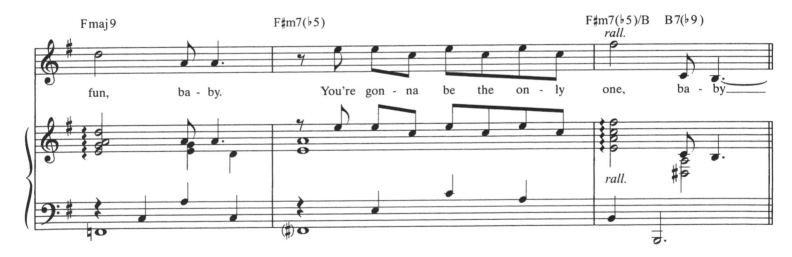

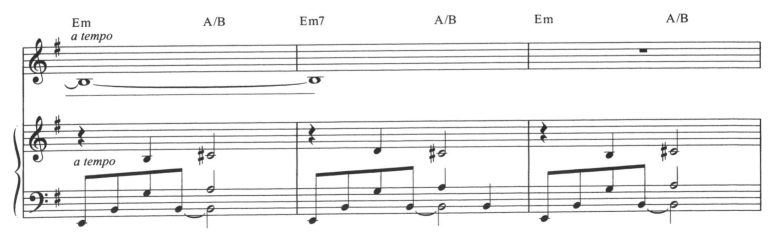

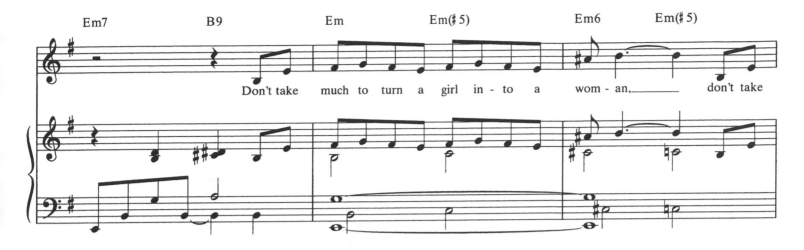

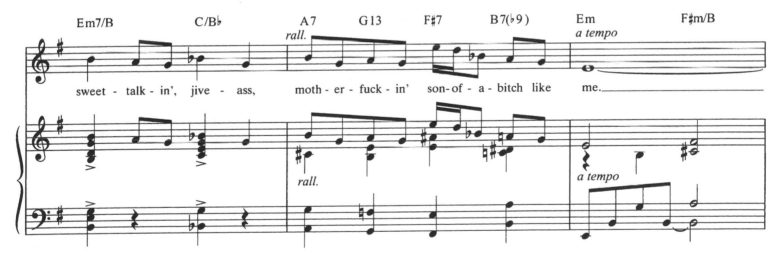

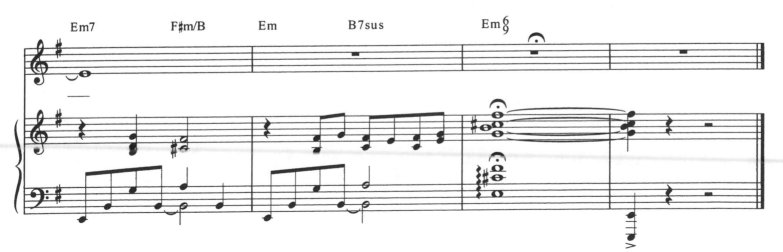

YOU CAN'T GET TO HEAVEN

Music by CY COLEMAN
Lyrics by IRA GASMAN

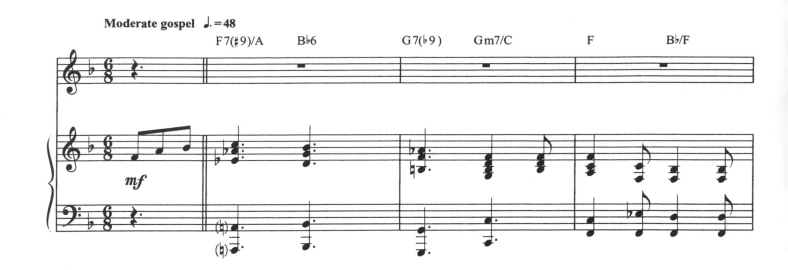

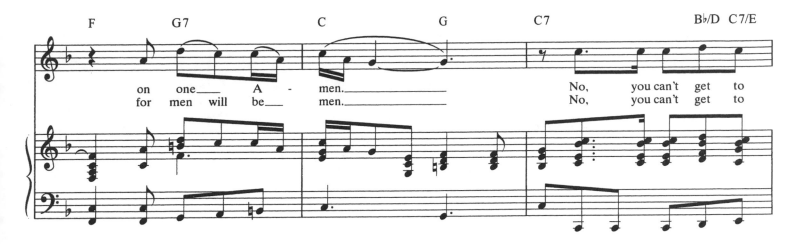

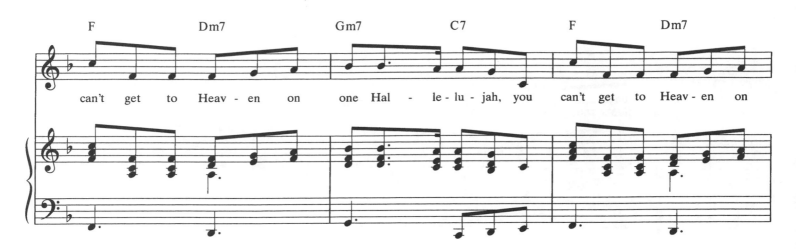

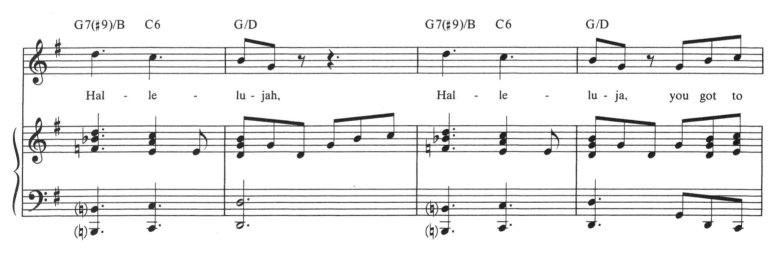

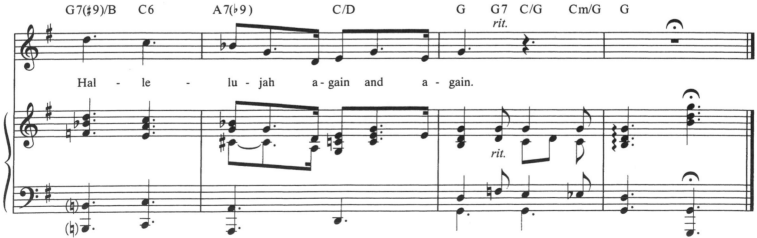

MY BODY

Music by CY COLEMAN
Lyrics by IRA GASMAN

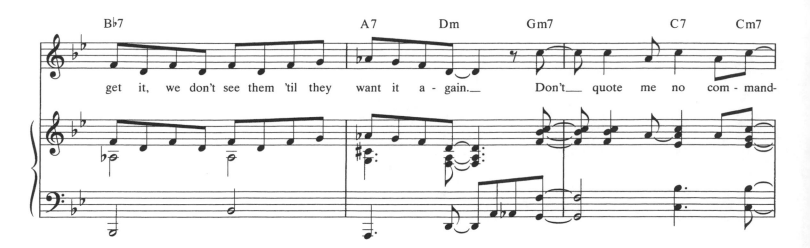

get it, we don't see them 'til they want it a-gain.__ Don't__ quote me no com-mand-

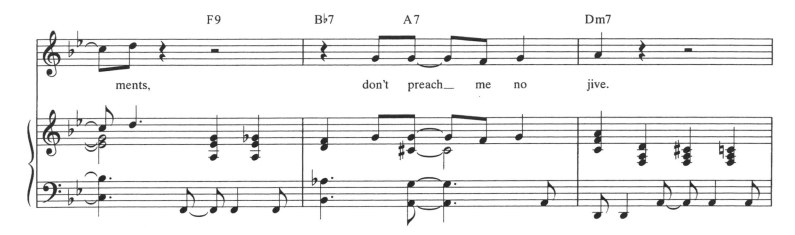

ments, don't preach__ me no jive.

There's on-ly one com-mand-ment: "Thou shalt sur-vive."__

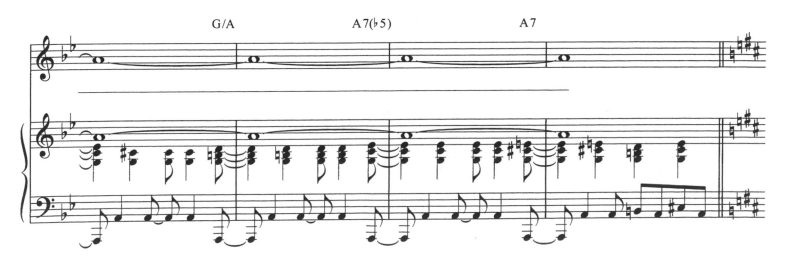

Chorus:

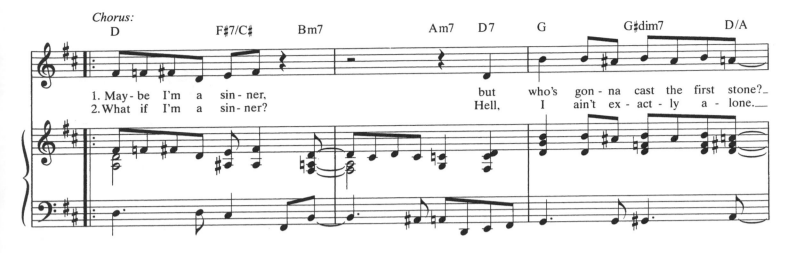

1. May-be I'm a sin-ner, but who's gon-na cast the first stone?_
2. What if I'm a sin-ner? Hell, I ain't ex-act-ly a - lone._

It's my bod - y, and my bod - y's

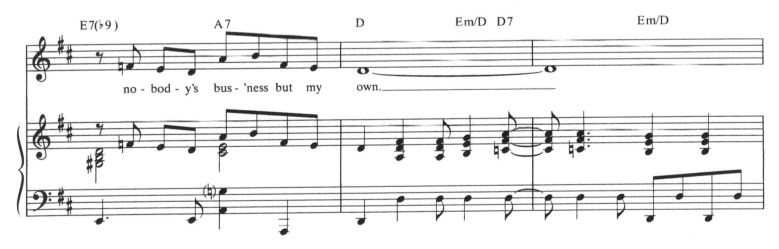

no - bod - y's bus - 'ness but my own._

44

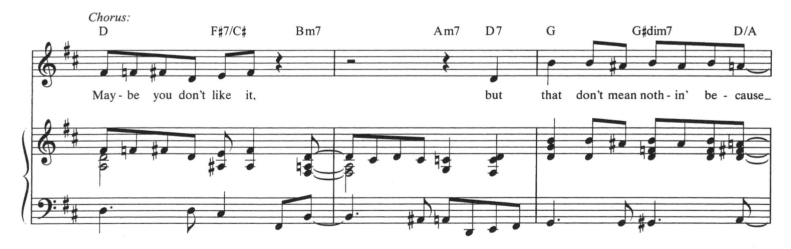

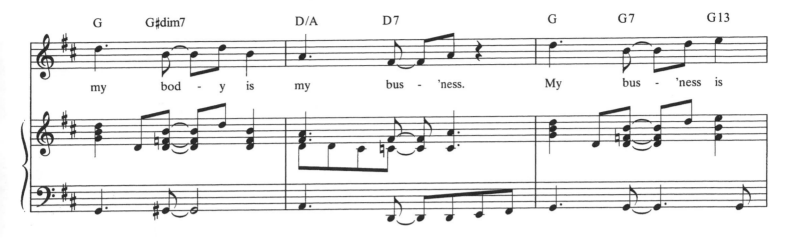

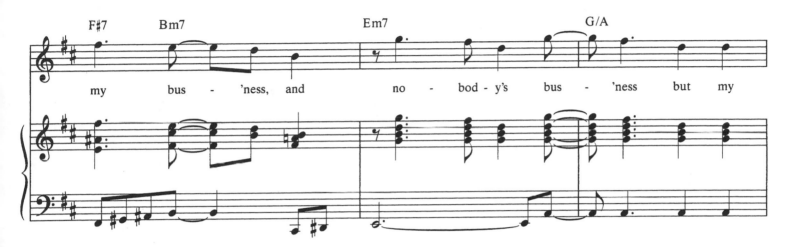

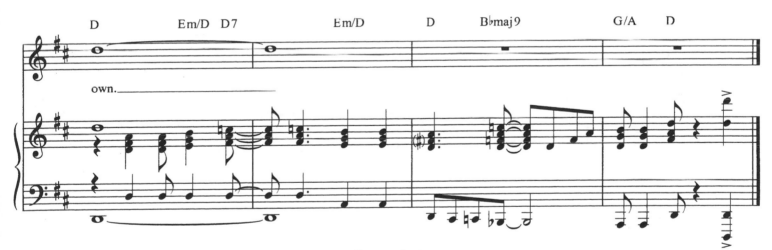

Alternate Lyrics

Verse:
I've had it up to here with all your "holier than thou's"
Who want to save me from the devil's wicked den.
Quit shoutin' in my ear with all your curses and your vows,
I only wish I never had to hear your voices again.
Don't quote me no commandments, don't preach me no jive.
There's only one commandment: "Thou shalt survive."

Chorus 1:
Listen to me people
'Cause I wanna let it be known.
It's my body, and my body's
Nobody's business but my own.

Chorus 2:
I know what I'm doing,
So why don't you leave me alone?
It's my body, and my body's
Nobody's business but my own.

Bridge:
I'm a grown-up woman
And I know who I am.
If you've got a problem,
I don't give a damn.

Chorus 3:
Ain't no doubt about it
'Cause, baby, it's written in stone.
It's my body, not your body,
And my body is my business.
My business is my business,
And nobody's business but my own.

WHY DON'T THEY LEAVE US ALONE

Music by CY COLEMAN
Lyrics by IRA GASMAN

leave us work - ing girls__ a - lone?__ Why don't they leave us
leave us bus - 'ness men__ a - lone?__ Why don't they leave us

work - ing girls__ a - lone?_____ We're
bus - 'ness men__ a - lone?_____ The

tired of get - tin' bust - ed by those men in blue.__ We're on - ly out there do - in' what we
pad - dy wag - on's jump - in' but the street is dead.__ And once a - gain we're op - er - at - in'

got - ta do.__ How come they nev - er bust the guys we do it to?__ Why don't they
in the red.__ So how are we sup - posed to meet our o - ver - head?__ Why don't they

leave us work - ing girls___ a - lone?___ Why don't they leave us
leave us bus - 'ness men___ a - lone?___ Why don't they leave us

work - ing girls___ a - lone? Why don't they leave us a - lone?___ The
bus - 'ness men___ a - lone? Why don't they leave us a - lone?___ Yes,

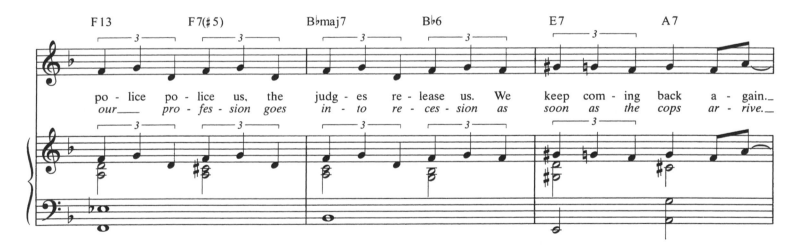

po - lice po - lice us, the judg - es re - lease us. We keep com - ing back a - gain.___
our___ pro - fes - sion goes in - to re - ces - sion as soon as the cops ar - rive.___

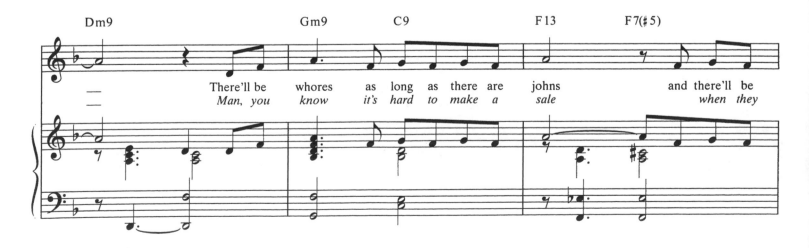

___ There'll be whores as long as there are johns and there'll be
___ Man, you know it's hard to make a sale when they

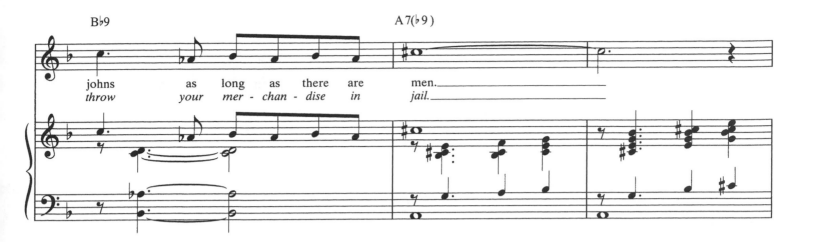

johns as long as there are men._____
throw your mer - chan - dise in jail._____

The cops are al - ways there no mat - ter
The cops are get - tin' off by get - tin'

where we're at.__ They trail us and they tail us and they nail us flat.__ And
on our case.__ There're down our necks or on our backs or in our face.__ What

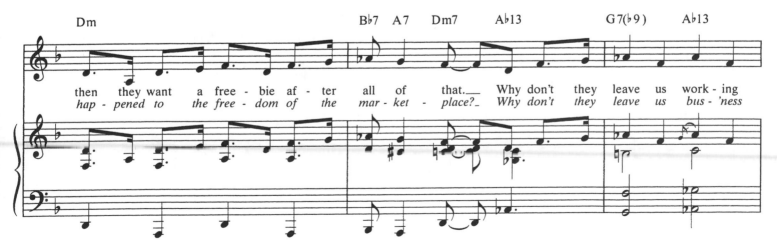

then they want a free - bie af - ter all of that.__ Why don't they leave us work - ing
hap - pened to the free - dom of the mar - ket - place?__ Why don't they leave us bus - 'ness

girls_____ a - lone?_____   Why don't they leave us
men_____ a - lone?_____   Why don't they leave us

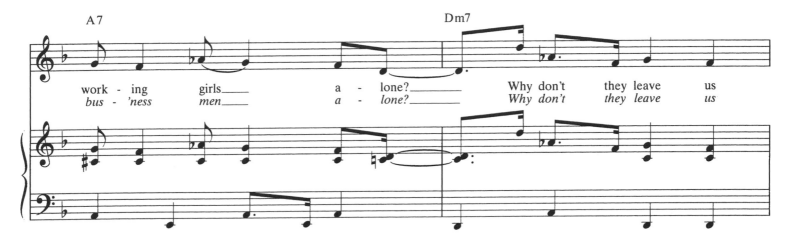

work - ing girls_____ a - lone?_____   Why don't they leave us
bus - 'ness men_____ a - lone?_____   Why don't they leave us

work - ing girls_____ a - lone?_____   Why don't they, why don't they,
bus - 'ness men_____ a - lone?_____   Why don't they, why don't they,

why don't they, why don't they,   why don't they leave us a - lone?_____
why don't they, why don't they,   why don't they leave us a - lone?_____

EASY MONEY

Music by CY COLEMAN
Lyrics by IRA GASMAN

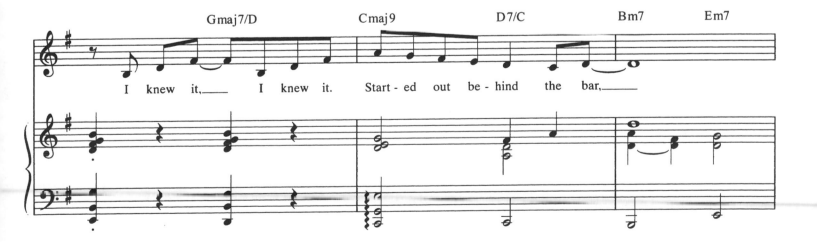

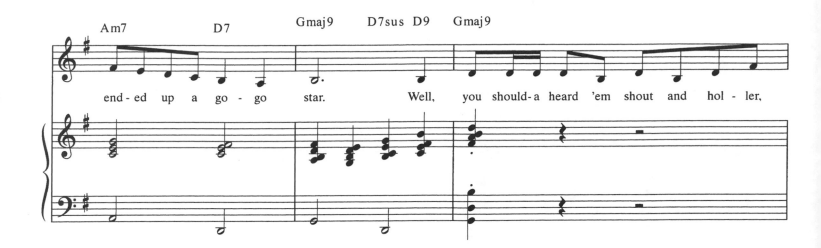

Am7   D7   Gmaj9   D7sus   D9   Gmaj9

end-ed up a go - go star.   Well, you should-a heard 'em shout and hol - ler,

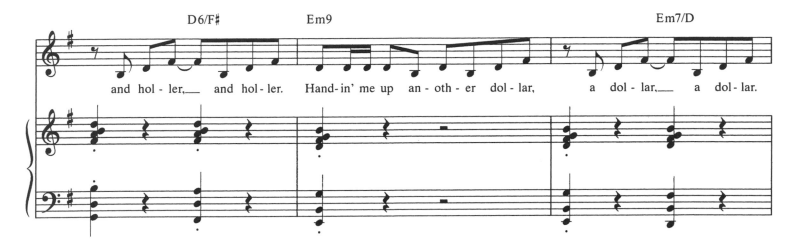

D6/F♯   Em9   Em7/D

and hol - ler,___ and hol - ler. Hand-in' me up an - oth - er dol - lar,   a dol - lar,___ a dol - lar.

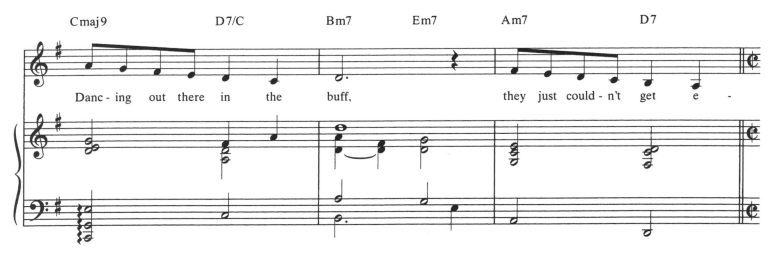

Cmaj9   D7/C   Bm7   Em7   Am7   D7

Danc - ing out there in the buff,   they just could - n't get e -

G   F♯+   G   F♯+

nough of   me.___   An - y - one___ who was there___ would - a seen___ why

Told ya, kid,___   I'd be fine.___ Now ya see___ things are break - in'.

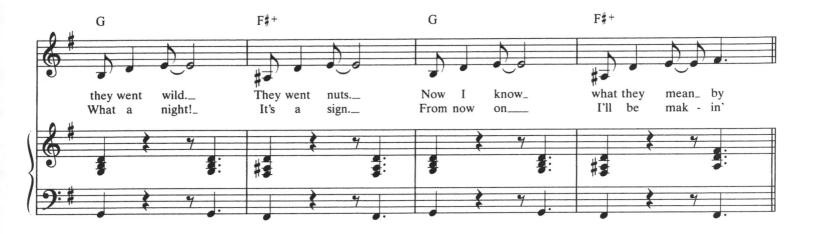

they went wild.___ They went nuts.___ Now I know___ what they mean___ by
What a night!___ It's a sign.___ From now on___ I'll be mak - in'

eas - y mon - ey;
eas - y mon - ey;
I'm learn - ing how to make___ it.
to - mor - row, let's go shop - pin'.

Eas - y mon - ey, you just reach out and take___ it.
Eas - y mon - ey, we'll keep that sales girl hop - pin'.

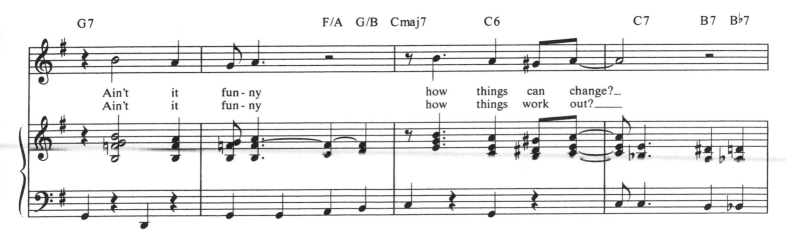

Ain't it fun - ny how things can change?___
Ain't it fun - ny how things work out?_____

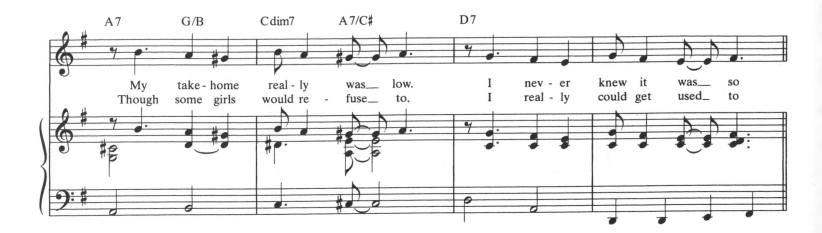

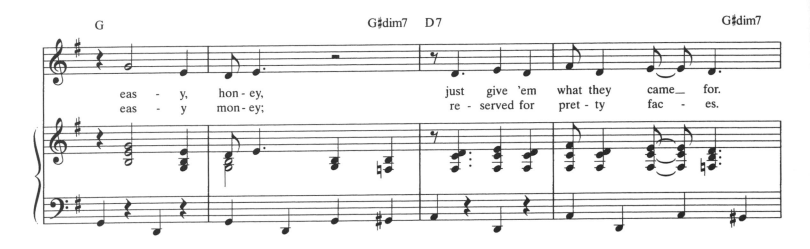

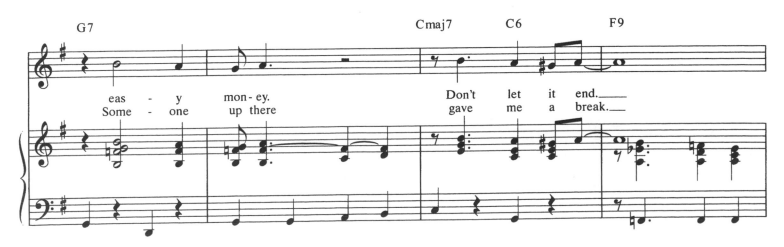

HE'S NO GOOD

Music by CY COLEMAN
Lyrics by IRA GASMAN

58

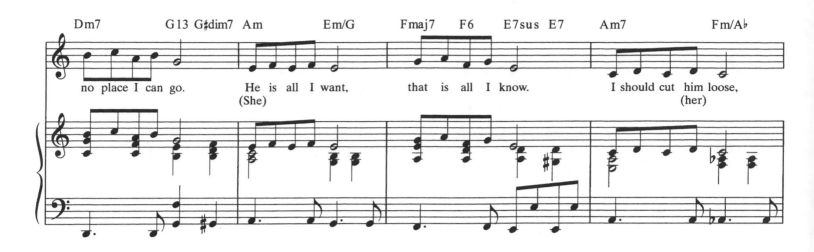

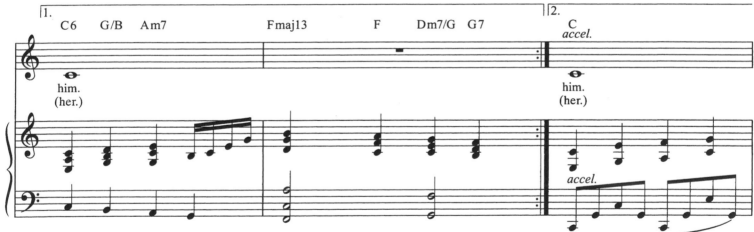

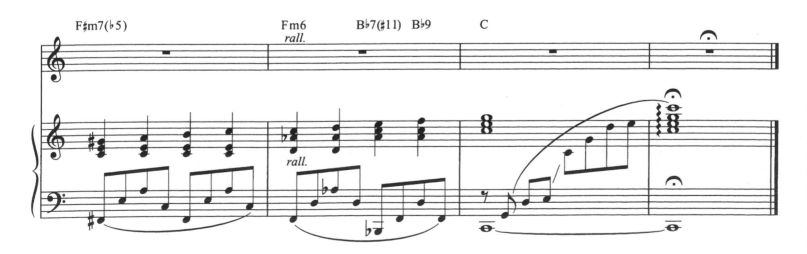

I'M LEAVING YOU

Music by CY COLEMAN
Lyrics by IRA GASMAN

leav-ing you._____ What ev - er hap-pened to that dream we used to

share? What ev - er hap-pened to the love that once was there? What ev - er

hap - pened to me and you?_____

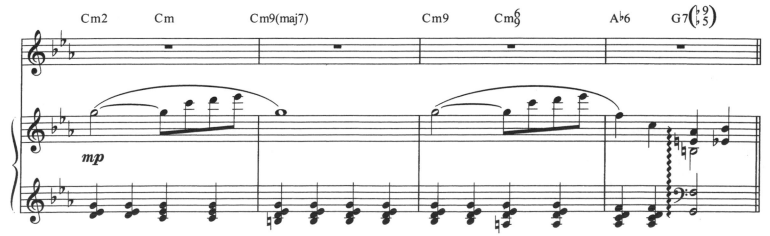

HOOKER'S BALL

Music by CY COLEMAN
Lyrics by IRA GASMAN

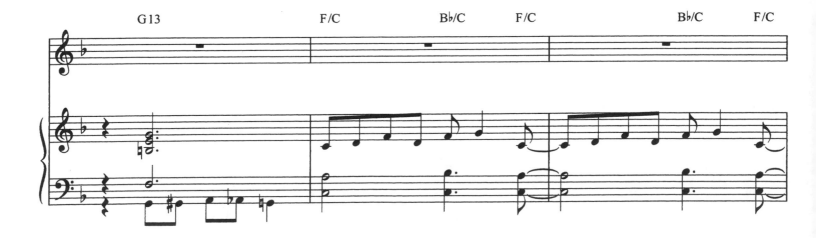

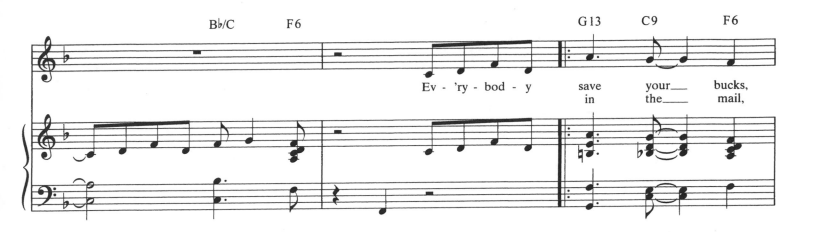

Ev - 'ry - bod - y save your___ bucks,
in the___ mail,

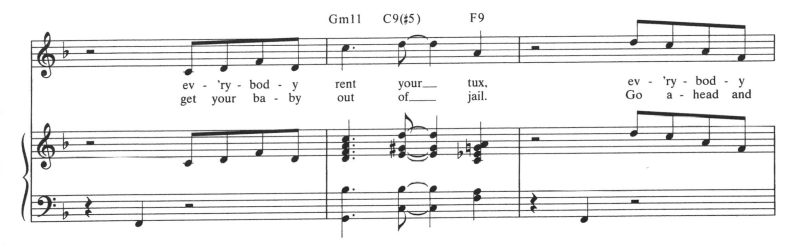

ev - 'ry - bod - y rent your___ tux,
get your ba - by out of___ jail.
ev - 'ry - bod - y
Go a - head and

dress de - luxe, we're
make her___ bail, you're
go - in' to the hook - er's ball.___
go - in' to the hook - er's ball.___

In - vi - ta - tions ___
We're gon - na eat and drink___ and be

64

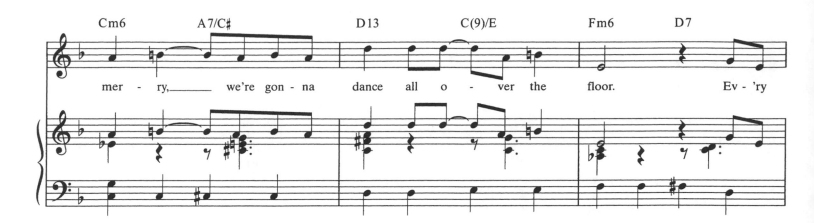

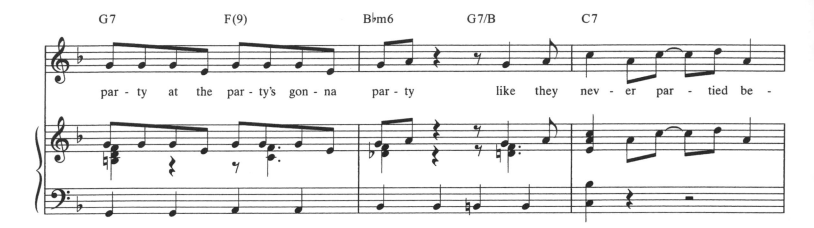

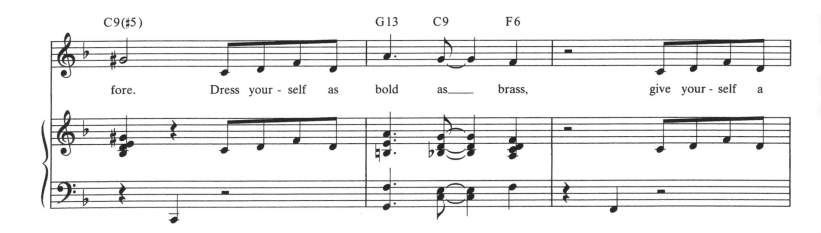

we're go - in' to the hook - er's ball.

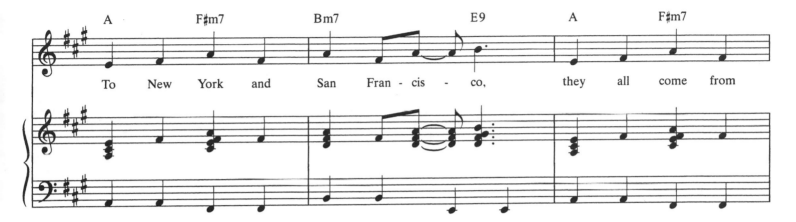

To New York and San Fran - cis - co, they all come from

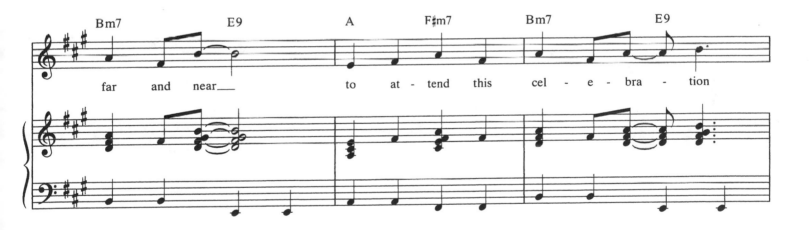

far and near___ to at - tend this cel - e - bra - tion

that is held one night a year.___ On - ly those in

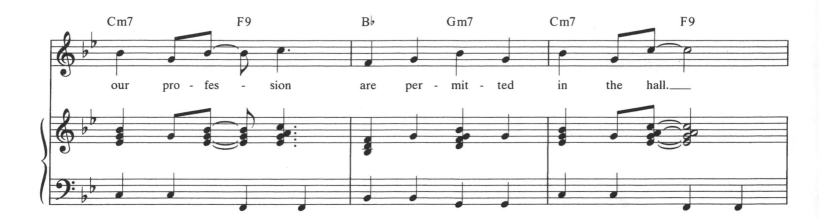

our pro - fes - sion   are per - mit - ted   in the hall.____

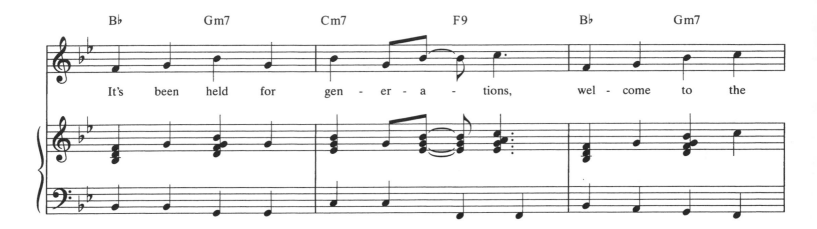

It's   been   held   for   gen - er - a - tions,   wel - come   to   the

hook - er's   ball.____   How   they   dress   will   knock   you   out____   and

wake   you   up   a - gain.____   The   dia - monds   shine,   the

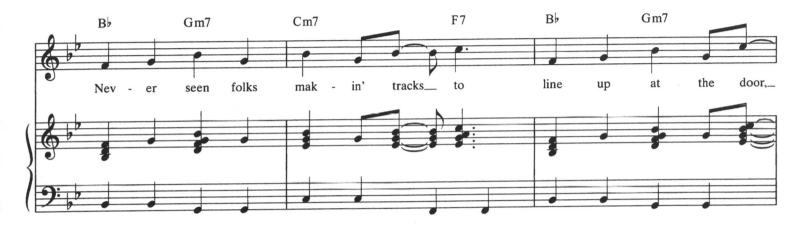

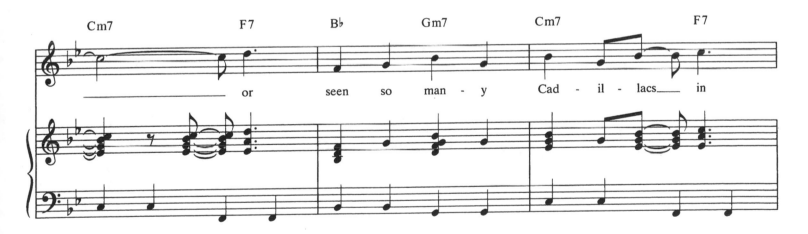

bust - in' loose,___ a great big free for all_____ and

Moderate swing ♩ = 96

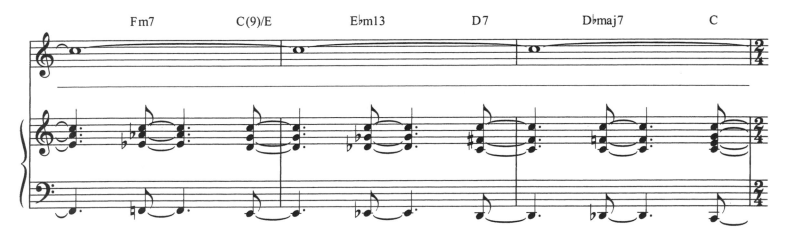

though there is no Moth - er Goose___ there real - ly is a hook - er's ball.___

Tempo I

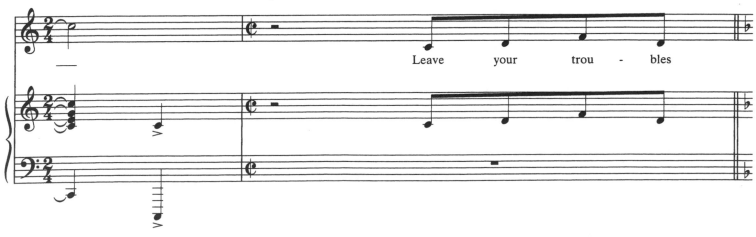

Leave your trou - bles

at the____ door,   they will trou - ble you no____ more.
at - mos - phere.   Ba - by, ain't you glad you're__ here?

Stay un - til your feet get____ sore, you're
It's the par - ty of the____ year, we're

danc - in' at the hook - er's ball.____ Ba - by, dig the ___ We're gon - na
talk - in' 'bout the hook - er's ball.__

eat and drink__ and be mer - ry,_____ we're gon - na dance all o - ver the

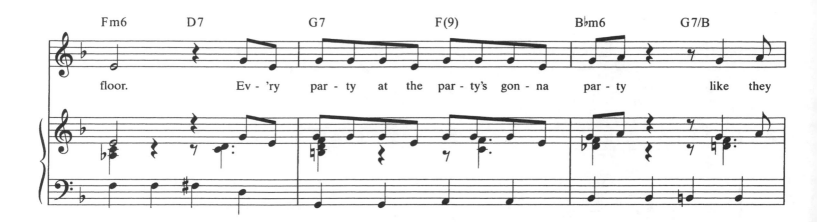

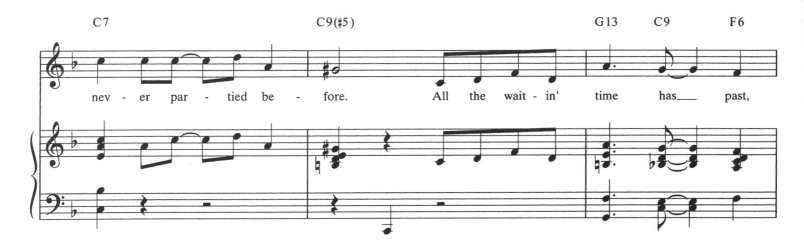

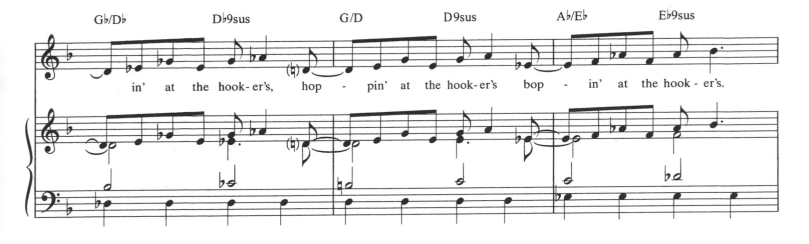

in' at the hook-er's, hop - pin' at the hook-er's bop - in' at the hook-er's.

Wel - come to the hook - er's ball._____

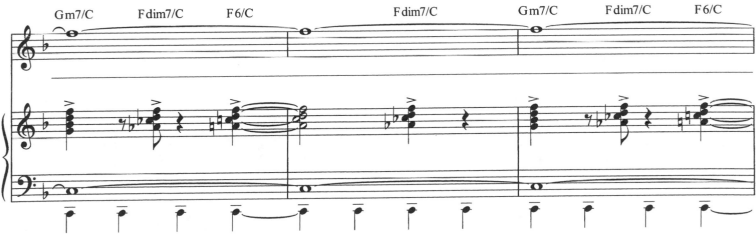

8vb

MR. GREED

Music by CY COLEMAN
Lyrics by IRA GASMAN

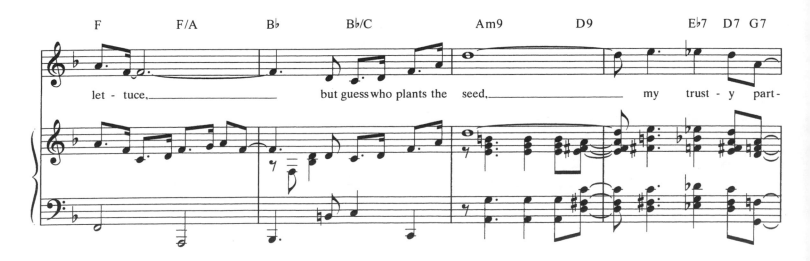

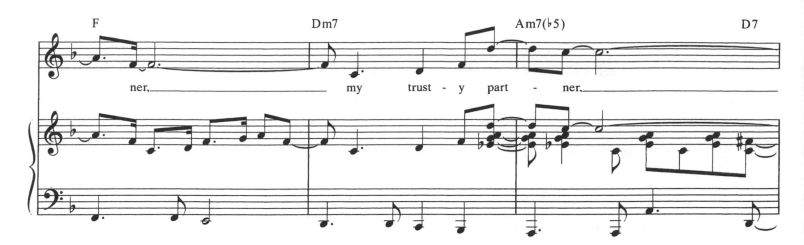

ner,_____ my trust - y part - ner,_____

___ me and my part - ner,_____ Mis - ter Greed._

MY WAY OR THE HIGHWAY

Music by CY COLEMAN
Lyrics by IRA GASMAN

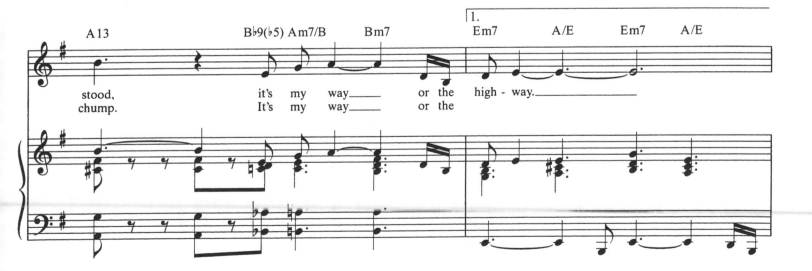

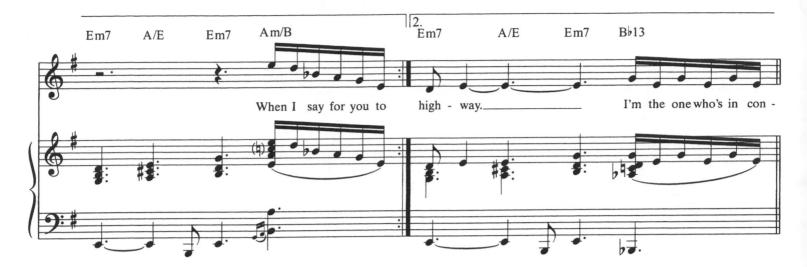

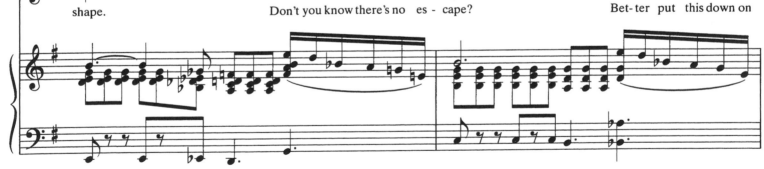

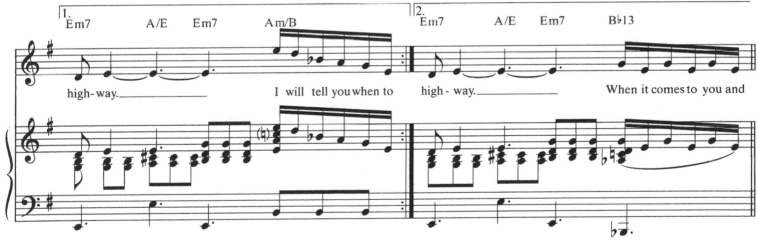

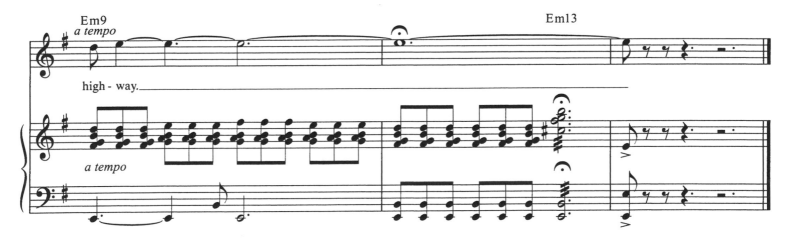

Alternate Lyrics

Listen girl and listen good.
You ain't doin' like you should.
Let's get one thing understood,
It's my way or the highway.

My way simply don't allow
Breaking every single vow.
Make your mind up here and now.
It's my way or the highway.

There's one thing I'm certain of;
I ain't gonna share your love.

Bet you think you're pretty smart
Playing falsely with my heart.
Time to make a brand new start.
It's my way or the highway.

There's one thing I'm certain of;
I ain't gonna share your love.

Time to get your act in shape.
I ain't gonna bow or scrape.
Better put this down on tape:
It's my way or the highway.
My way or the highway.

PEOPLE MAGAZINE

Music by CY COLEMAN
Lyrics by IRA GASMAN

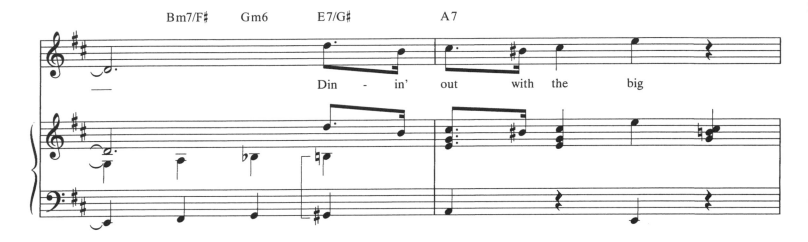

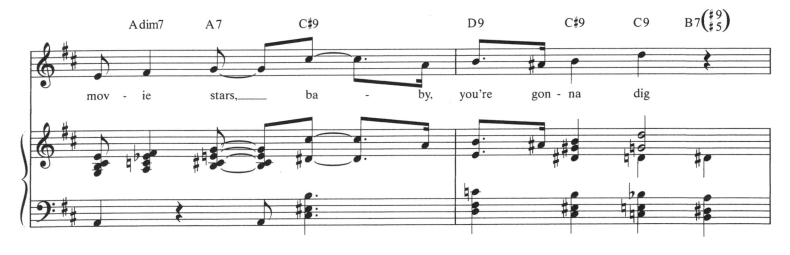

hind the di - vid - er in - side a lim - ou - sine,___

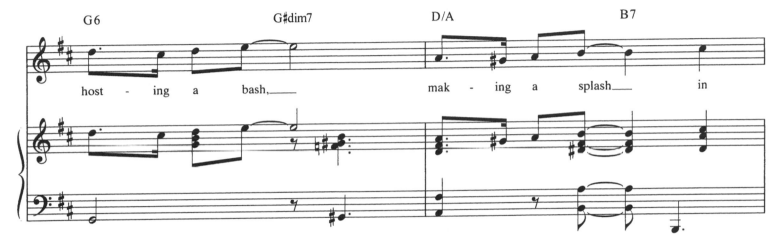

host - ing a bash,___ mak - ing a splash___ in

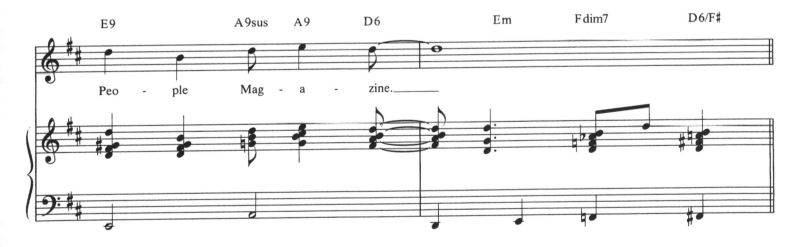

Peo - ple Mag - a - zine.___

Come with me and you can go as far as your tal - ent

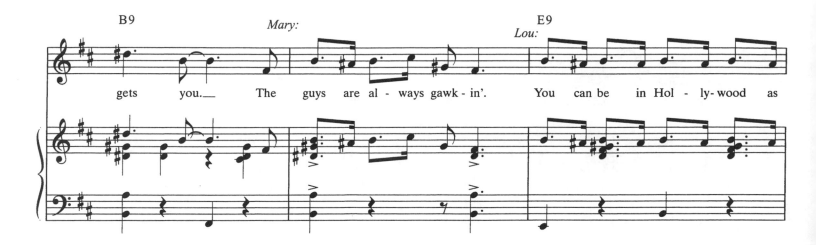

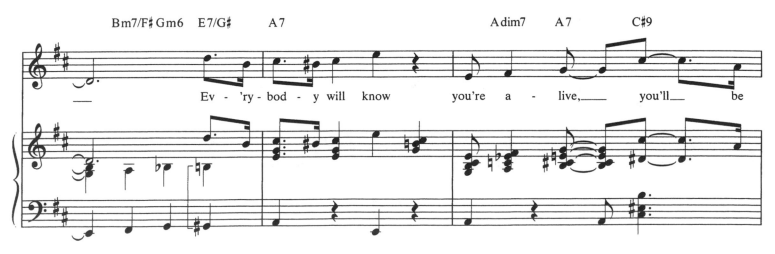

far as your tal - ent gets you.___

to L. A. There's noth - ing here to hold me.

You can be in Hol - ly-wood as fast as a Boe - ing jets you.___

What more can I say?

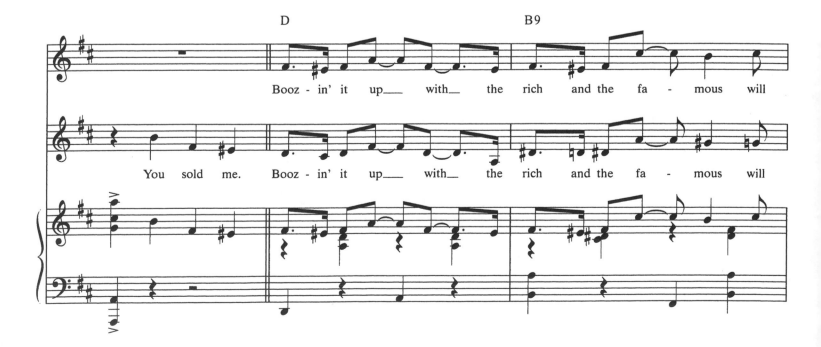

Booz - in' it up___ with___ the rich and the fa - mous will

You sold me. Booz - in' it up___ with___ the rich and the fa - mous will

Bright two-beat ($\dot{} = 152$)

Peo - ple Mag - a -

zine?

Peo - ple Mag - a -

zine?

8vb

WE HAD A DREAM

Music by CY COLEMAN
Lyrics by IRA GASMAN

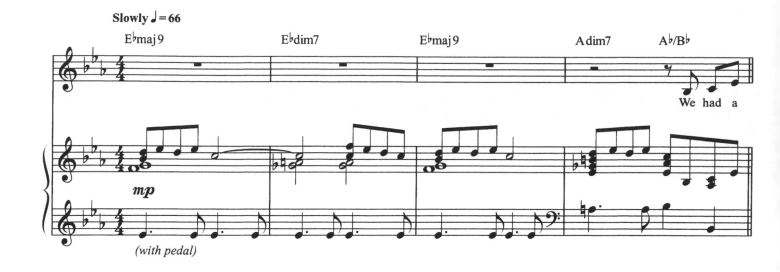

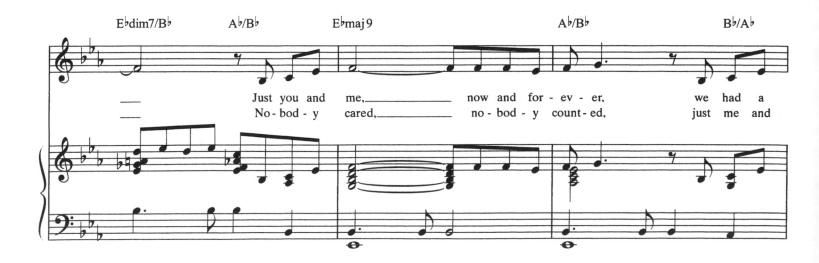

Alternate Lyrics

We had a dream, don't you remember?
We had a dream.
Just you and me now and forever,
We had a dream.
Make a little magic every day.
Never let the magic go away.
Right from the start, don't you remember?
We had a dream.

{ You were my man, I was your woman. }
{ *I was your man, you were my woman.* }
That's all we knew.
Nobody cared, nobody counted,
Just me and you.
Could it be you've had a change of heart?
Was I really dreaming from the start?
Is it really time to say goodbye?
Doesn't love deserve another try?
We had a dream,
We had a dream,
Don't let it die.

SOMEDAY IS FOR SUCKERS

Music by CY COLEMAN
Lyrics by IRA GASMAN

Fm9

sick of wait-in' while some bas-tard looks me o - ver, stand-ing there de - cid-ing yes or no.
sick and tired of feel - ing like my back is bro - ken, sick of get-ting splint-ers in my knees.

Cm(9)

Sick of ev-'ry dick, of ev-'ry hot and sweat-y trick who says "How much" be-fore he e - ven says "Hel-lo."
Sick of be-ing wor-ried if I'm gon-na catch a beat-ing, not to men-tion catch-ing who-knows-what dis - ease.

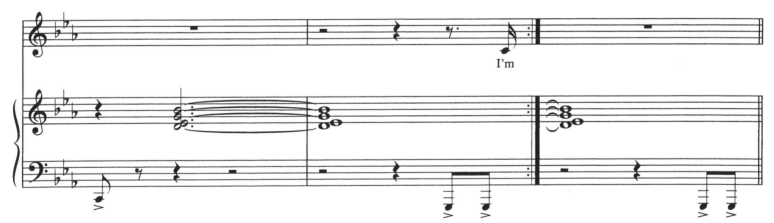

1.　　　　　　　　　2.

I'm

Cm(9)

Frenchie:

Some-day I'll be work-in' in a mil-lion dol-lar pent-house where my tricks-'ll all be com-in' to me.__

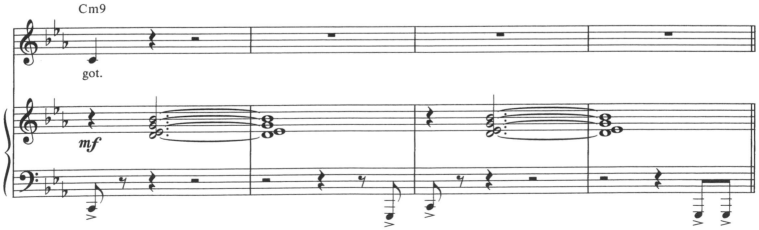

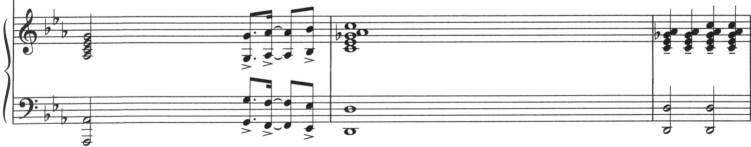

MY FRIEND

Music by CY COLEMAN
Lyrics by IRA GASMAN

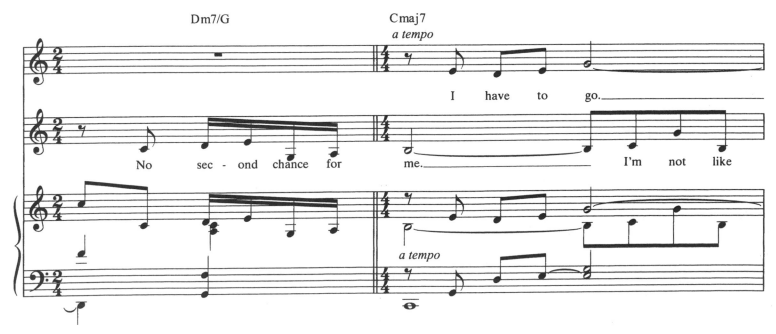

WE GOTTA GO

Music by CY COLEMAN
Lyrics by IRA GASMAN

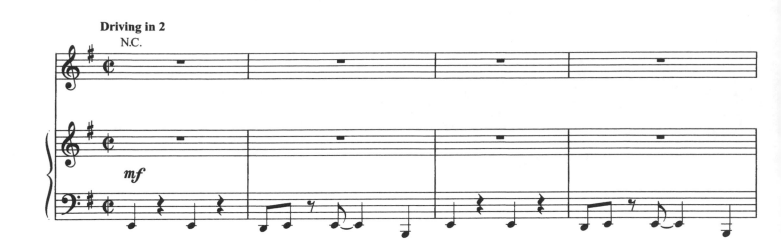

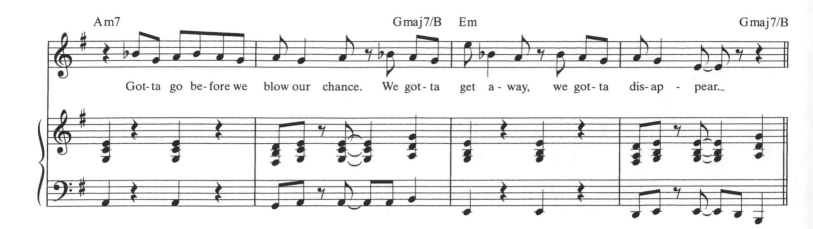

Got-ta go be-fore we blow our chance. We got-ta get a - way, we got-ta dis-ap - pear._

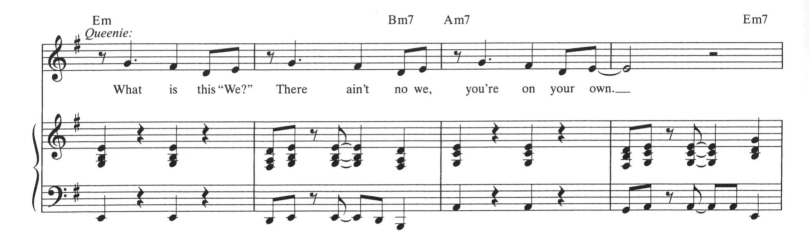

Queenie:
What is this "We?" There ain't no we, you're on your own._

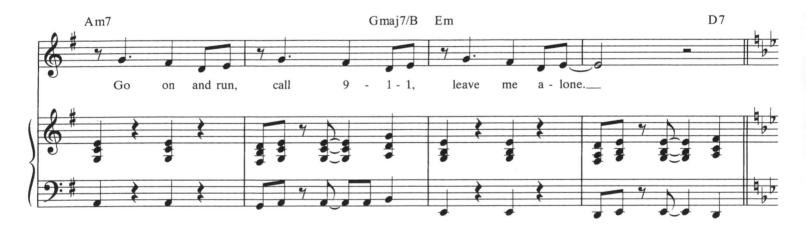

Go on and run, call 9 - 1 - 1, leave me a - lone._

You're like a sick - ness in my soul that nev - er passed._

Tempo I

(Q:) That was my mis-take.___ Go to Hell and take the past with you.___

(F:) Oh, ba-by,

Go on and beg but that won't get you an-y-where.___

please gim-me an-oth-er chance._ I nev-er

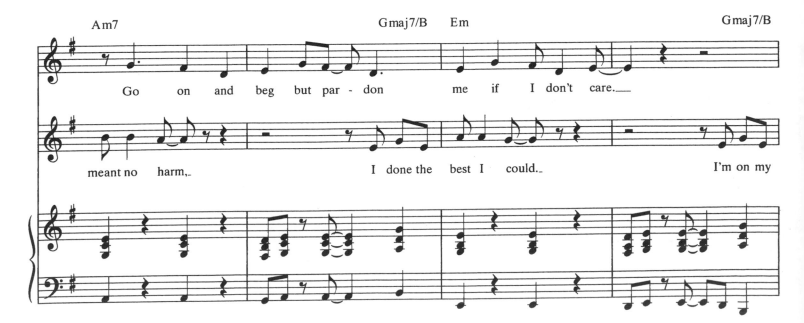

Go on and beg but par-don me if I don't care.___

meant no harm,_ I done the best I could._ I'm on my

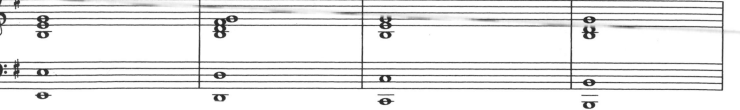

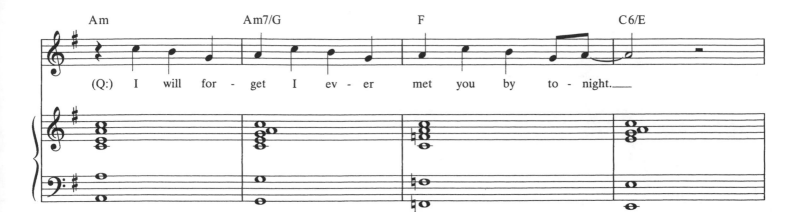

(Q:) I will for-get I ev-er met you by to-night.___

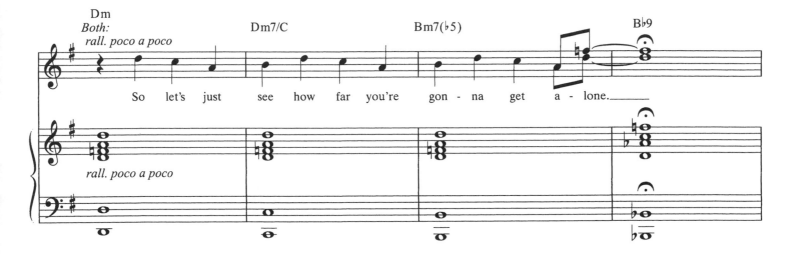

So let's just see how far you're gon-na get a-lone.___

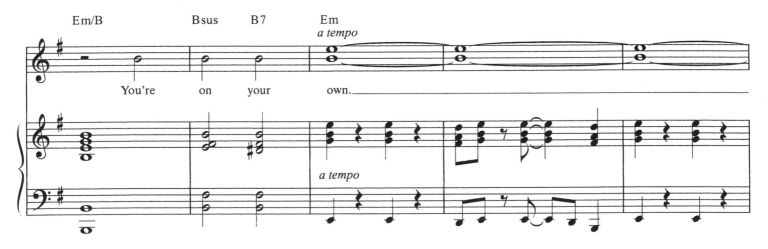

You're on your own.___